MW01284573

One, Two, Three!

A Collection of Songs, Verses, Riddles and Stories for Children of Grades 1–3

by David Adams

Waldorf
PUBLICATIONS
RESEARCH INSTITUTE FOR *Waldorf* EDUCATION

Printed with support from the Waldorf Curriculum Fund

Published by:

Waldorf Publications at the
Research Institute for Waldorf Education
38 Main Street
Chatham, NY 12037

Title: *One, Two, Three! A Collection of Songs, Verses, Riddles and Stories
for Children of Grades 1–3*
Author: David Adams
Editor: David Mitchell
Layout: Ann Erwin
Cover: Hallie Wootan
© 2002 by AWSNA
Revised edition 2017 © by Waldorf Publications
ISBN #978-1-888365-35-1

Curriculum Series

The Publications Committee of the Research Institute is pleased to bring forward this publication as part of its Curriculum Series. The thoughts and ideas represented herein are solely those of the author and do not necessarily represent any implied criteria set by Waldorf Publications. It is our intention to stimulate as much writing and thinking as possible about our curriculum, including diverse views. Please contact us at patrice@waldorf-research.org with feedback on this publication as well as requests for future work.

Contents

Preface

For the most part, the materials in this collection speak for themselves. Nearly all were composed by me in the course of work as a class teacher or music teacher in several Waldorf schools. A few others arose in connection with parenting duties as a housefather at a small boarding home in Denver from 1973 to 1974 or as stepfather to two dear girls during the later 1970s and early 1980s. I also include a handful of pieces written by my teaching colleagues that have proved most popular with children in my classes. All but one or two pieces have been "child-tested," most with several groups of children over a number of years.

The material gathered here is directed toward a particular period in child development, those few precious years when the child is no longer in the largely imitative, movement-oriented phase of the first six or seven years of life nor yet quite on the other side of that "great divide" of the "nine-year-old change" (after which the child experiences a sharper distinction between self and world, or inner and outer experience). A new imaginative or pictorial thinking has come gradually to birth around the beginning of the change of teeth, and the child is hungry for mental images to work with. At the same time a new blossoming of the feeling life is tied to a natural affinity with rhythm of all kinds. It is between the twin pillars of imagination and rhythm that most of the following verses, songs, riddles and stories find their home.

I have felt motivated to share these pieces primarily as examples of the kind of materials especially suited to children in grades one through three. My hope is that they will stimulate others to create their own verses, songs, and stories for specific groups of children. There is nothing more effective, either in educating or parenting, than something adults have created themselves and can present to children as a personal gift filled with the afterglow of their own inner work and life energy.

This is actually more important pedagogically than the poetic, musical or literary refinement of what is created (although the latter is not unimportant). That said, anyone who has taught young children knows that the time to create one's own classroom material is not always available. For such situations the following examples may provide a welcome addition to the material the teacher can draw upon to prepare lessons. Songs, verses and stories are listed in a loose order, progressing more or less from material for younger children to pieces more suited for older ones.

I would also like to acknowledge here the warm inspiration I received for composing these pieces early on in my Waldorf teaching career from Elisabeth Lebret, Helmut von Kugelgen, Werner Glas, and Diethart Jaehnig. In addition, I and anyone else who appreciates the boundless insight into child development and the enormous practical pedagogical wisdom that lie behind Waldorf education must be forever grateful to its far-seeing founder, Rudolf Steiner.

David Adams
Penn Valley, California
April 2002

Verses

These verses were primarily composed in a Waldorf school context as recitation or movement exercises to help get a group of children "breathing together" at the beginning of a lesson or school day. The rhythmic alternation between large and small, loud and soft, movement and rest, fast and slow, or expansion and contraction can become like a kind of psychological "breathing" that works, among other things, to gather and focus the scattered energies and attentions of the class before a more academic lesson begins. Some of these pieces include suggestions for accompanying movements, and teachers are encouraged to devise their own pictorial movements to be performed by the teacher (and imitated by the children) for each verse. (See the more complete explanation for this in the introductory comments to the "Songs" section.)

Circle Gathering Verse

In the circle (first) grade stands,
Quiet mouths and quiet hands,
Feet together, standing straight as can be
While (teacher) counts, "One, two, three!"

The Train

Choo! Choo! Choo!	(Briskly rub open palms together vertically.)
The train goes down the track.	("Walk" two fingers from shoulder down arm.)
Choo! Choo! Choo!	(as before)
And then it goes right back.	("Walk" two fingers from wrist up to shoulder.)
Choo! Choo! Choo!	(as before)
Those wheels are turning fast!	(Rapidly whirl hands around each other.)
Choo! Choo! Choo!	(as before)
I hear a train go past.	(Cup hand to ear and listen.)
Whoo! Whoo!	(Speak into cupped hand to give whistle effect.)

Short Verses for Expansion-Contraction Movements in a Circle
(movements into the center and back again to the circumference)

Into the pond the frogs do go;	(Try hopping in like frogs.)
Out and out the ripples flow.	(Arms and fingers make rippling movements.)
The birds soar high into the sky,	(Make wing movements with arms while
And back into their nest they fly.	walking into and back out from the circle.)
I bring my light so deep inside	(intended for late autumn or winter)
That it may shine out far and wide.	
Let's creep into our little cave	(to be accompanied by a short
Where we'll be safe and warm,	story image of bears looking for a
But run back out so very fast	cave in which to hibernate and
Before the bees can swarm.	encountering a beehive inside)

Isn't Straight Nice?

Up, down, without a sound,	*(Move heels of feet up and down four*
Touch your ears twice.	*times in rhythm to the first two lines.)*
Lean back, lean front,	*(Keeping feet together in place,*
Isn't straight nice?	*lean slightly backward, then forward;*
	end standing straight.)

Our Class (accompanied by movements)

A large and lovely land are we
With stars above and flowing seas,
With rocks and trees and birds and beasts,
With far and near, and great and least,
With houses strong to keep us warm
And safe from snow and rain and storm,
With friends on every side around,
Full of love, we stand our ground.

Grapes

We are picking purple grapes	*(Pick imaginary grapes with arms and*
Ripened in the sun,	*hands.)*
Putting them in baskets	*(Put grape bunches in "basket" formed by*
Till our work is done.	*rounded left arm.)*
Then we squish them with our feet,	*(Mash grapes by twisting feet on floor.)*
Make some grape juice wet and sweet.	
If it ferments, wine is born;	*(open, rising fingers for fermentation gases)*
Or dry the grapes and raisins form.	*(Slowly close open hands to fists.)*
The best of grapes are ripe and sweet,	
Juicy-fresh, they're quite a treat!	*(Rub tummy.)*

Useful for children living too strongly in their imaginations or thinking processes, this "grape" verse moves from motions with raised hands at head level through rhythmic arm movements in the middle region (baskets) and then down to feet movements. Repeated, it should help bring such children more into their limbs and "down to earth." The following verse, inspired by a suggestion of Else Göttgens, works toward a similar result, but is perhaps more useful for gathering and calming the children to a wakefully present state of mind at the beginning of an activity.

Descent

The eagle soars in lofty skies.	*(vigorous flying movements with arms)*
The sea gull glides both low and high.	*(somewhat less vigorous, "gliding" movements)*
The sparrow lifts small wings to fly.	*(flying movements with just wrists and hands)*
The angel silently floats nigh,	*(Bring arms from behind toward front in a rounded, protective gesture.)*
And standing here below am I.	*(Stand up straight with feet together and arms crossed on the chest.)*

Upward Growth

From down below	*(Stand slouched with head down.)*
Up I grow	*(Rise up straight.)*
And spread my leaves out wide.	*(Extend arms out to sides.)*
Above I form a little room	*(Raise and cup hands above the head.)*
From which the lovely flower bloom	*(Begin to spread open hands.)*
Opens to the huge sky.	*(Extend arms wide apart above the head.)*

This is the opposite gesture to "Grapes." It is helpful to first give the child a verbal imagination of a plant growing and flowering. The "little room" is the calyx. This verse is useful for a child who needs to bring wakeful or skillful limb/ will forces up into the head, whose activity may be weaker or too intellectual.

Orientation

Below is the earth	*(Lower arms and hands toward ground.)*
Above is the sky	*(Raise arms and hands up in the air.)*
There are my friends	*(Extend arms horizontally with open palms.)*
And here am I.	*(Stand straight, feet together, as arms cross over the chest.)*

Morning Warm-Up

I touch the sky,	*(Raise hands up high.)*
I touch my feet,	*(Touch feet with both hands, knees straight.)*
I clap my hands	*(Turn 360° in place, clapping hands to stressed syllables of*
On every beat.	*verse.)*
Without a sound	*(Turn 360° in place again, but no clapping.)*
I turn around,	
And this new day	*(Greet the day and the class by bringing bent arms out from*
I humbly greet.	*the chest, straightening arms forward and down with open*
	palms, while slightly bowing the head.)

Michaelmas Verse

Sword of Michael, brightly gleaming,
Down to earth its light is streaming.
May we see its shining rays
Through the winter's darkest days.

Winter Wisdom

The speech of the stars
Bright and lucid rings,
Fashions stars of ice
In the architecture of snow.
Clear sun-rays are shed
Deep in the winter of earth
To bear Nature's crystal wisdom
Into the heart of sleeping life.

Gratitude (accompanied by appropriate movements)

To stones at rest around their roots,
To soil that feeds their tender shoots,
The plants bend low in many ranks
To offer up their humble thanks.
To green and growing plants and trees,
To apples, carrots, grains, and peas,
The animals bend low their shanks
And offer up their humble thanks.
To beasts of water, air, and land,
To plants that all around us stand,
To rocks so firm beneath our feet,
We all give thanks and humbly greet.

Hippity Hippity Hop

Hippity hippity hop heigh ho!
[A-dancing] off to school we go
Down the road for half a mile,
It's not too far if you [dance] and smile.
Hippity hippity hop.
Trippity trippity light and neat,
Hark to the patter of dancing feet.
Trippity trippity down the lane,
Fairies a-frolicking out in the lane.

This is a verse given me by Class Teacher, Vanya Voors, from the Cape Ann Waldorf School. I have used it with his permission, although I have adapted it in certain ways. My version uses only the first verse and substitutes a series of varying movements for the words in brackets [e.g., A-skipping, A-running, A-tip-toeing, A-hopping, etc.], which the children perform around the circumference of the circle. For a variation (if you are brave), let the children perform the movements anywhere in the room, not only around the circle.

Evening Table Grace

Spirit within and spirit without,
Spirit in Nature round about,
Spirit that weaves through everything,
Thanks and praise to you we bring
For light of sun and warmth of earth
That take the seeds and give them birth
To grow the fruits and grains and leaves
That bless our table on this eve.

Bedtime Prayer

God so bright in heaven above,
Thank you for your boundless love,
For all the blessings of this day
That you have showered on my way;
Now send your angel, shining bright,
To stand beside me through the night,
To watch and guard me all night long
And keep me safe from harm and wrong.

The Birds on Good Friday

The birds on Good Friday are sweet'ning the air
With minstrelsy, madrigals, melodies rare,

Dear messages seeming, from out of the deep,
Deep blue of the firmament, voices from sleep,

Like voices of cherubim, choirs of love,
Celestial musicians, the wren and the dove.

Angelic the light that seems spun through their song,
To lift up our heart and to make our soul strong.

Riddles

Riddles can be helpful, among other things, for stimulating those children who do not live strongly enough in their imagination and mental imagery. Such children are eager to take up the challenge of solving the riddles, but they will be able to figure them out only through active mental picturing. In general, these riddles also exercise children's abilities to create relationships between visual observation, mental picturing, and verbal description. In addition to these practical purposes, riddles are fun!

I recommend that these mostly rhyming riddles be sung (preferably to an improvised pentatonic melody) and that the number of guesses be limited. I usually tell the answer after three guesses. The sometimes loose compositions of meter or measure, or the "forced" rhymes of many of these riddles require a bit of license and flexibility on the part of the speaker/singer. Most of these were written with eight-year-old children in mind, who have always been more than eager to try to solve them.

First I was yellow, I was yellow all right.
Then I was turned to snowy white.
I jumped and jumped, when I grew hot,
And the more I jumped, the bigger I got.   *(popcorn)*

Small and round, I curl up tight.
Green and closed, but soon I'll be bright.
I will spread my color out to the light.   *(flower bud)*

Five little sisters
Sitting on a hill:
They have hard little caps
And they bend at will.   *(fingers)*

Long and bent and soft,
We are just like each other.
We're two small warm houses
For five little brothers.   *(pair of socks or mittens)*

I'm hollow in my middle;
Can you guess this riddle?
But I'm thin
In my skin,
And all of me is skin.
I'm warm when you come in,
And my sister's always with me
To keep me company.   *(sock)*

I can stretch and twist like a snake
And hold things tight in my grasp.
But if I'm pulled too far,
I'll jump back with a snap!   *(rubber band)*

Big at the bottom,
Big at the top,
Long and thin in the middle.
I can roll on the ground,
And you can wind me up.
Now, can you guess this riddle?   *(a spool)*

Two arms have I
As I rock back and forth,
And though I have four legs,
I can't even walk out the door.   *(rocking chair)*

One little brother
After another,
All around the yard we go.
We are all just as tall
As each other
As we stand in a neat little row.   *(fence posts)*

Feathers in my tail,
A sharp, pointed nose;
Only the wind
Knows where I go.   *(arrow)*

Many tiny little holes
All in a row
Let the air inside,
But the bugs can't go.   *(screen)*

With a long, skinny body,
I have straight, blonde hair,
But people turn me upside down
And drag me everywhere.   *(broom)*

Close me up and shut out the light.
You close me up every night.   *(eyelids or curtains)*

You can't see the day when I come together.
I let you see the sun, moon, sky and weather.   *(curtains)*

I'll take you where you want to go.
If you go up or down, I know.
I go up and I go down;
Sometimes I even go around.   *(stairs)*

I'm thin and skinny
With shoulders wide.
I wear a shirt or pants
In which I hide.   *(hanger)*

I wear a black mask all around my eyes
Even though I only come out at night.
I have a soft stick with black and gray stripes. *(raccoon)*

I have more points than a nighttime star,
And I am golden and shining, too.
Always above you I will rest.
What's my name? Do you have a clue?   *(a crown)*

Round and round and round I go;
Though I move so very slow,
I have two arms but not a leg.
Try to guess me now, I beg.   *(clock)*

Two little sticks, each with pointed nose,
In and around and across it goes.
As we dance together, the larger it grows.   *(knitting needles)*

Round I go and never cease.
I have two hands that cannot seize.
I have a face without a nose,
Without two eyes — I'm one of those.   *(also a clock)*

Button me, button me, if you can.
You can find me on every man.
Like a little button or a button hole,
Wrinkled all up, I may make a bowl.   *(belly button, navel)*

Sometimes you can see right through me,
And sometimes you can't.
I have a neck and wear a little cap,
But my mouth can't sing or chant.   *(bottle)*

We all live in a long, green house
But stay as quiet as a mouse.
Many little sisters all in a row,
Feet of white, but heads of yellow.   *(corn)*

Though I'm made of sand and fire,
You can see right through me.
A man with skill can take and melt me down
And blow nice shapes into me.   *(glass)*

I'm a straight, sturdy blade
With a nice pointed tip,
But sometimes I get cut myself
With a clip, clip, clip.   *(blade of grass)*

Additional verse if hard to guess:

I'm straight and strong
Under the summer sky,
But when winter comes
I just about die.   *(blade of grass)*

I am a bed,
But I have no covers.
In the summertime
I show pretty colors.   *(flower bed)*

I have a broad back and a narrow belly.
I give children lots of fun.
But I have been to places
Where only birds have ever gone.   *(kite)*

First I'm a dragon, then I'm a bear.
Sometimes it seems I'm everywhere.
I turn blue to white,
But then, just for spite,
I pour all my buckets down there.   (cloud)

Like a whisk broom
Below the deep cave,
Fuzzy brown or black or gray,
It grows longer every day.   *(beard)*

I keep it warm, I keep it cold;
Take off my hat, use it to hold
What's in my fortress,
Round and bold.   *(thermos bottle)*

It flew through the air
While it whizzed and it whirled.
It looked like what your dinner's on
With sides bent down and curled.   (frisbee)

Rough, dark skin,
And when you go in,
It's soft and green
Around a big, hard bean.   (avocado)

I am a horse,
But you cannot ride me.
I don't have a head,
And I cannot see.   (sawhorse)

Tall am I, with a flat, pointed head;
Into the earth I dig my bed.   (shovel)

I'm always coming,
But I never arrive.
You keep heading for me
As long as you're alive.   (tomorrow)

I've a bright red cap
And a black and white suit.
I hammer on wood
With a tat-tat-tat-toot.   (red-headed woodpecker)

If you tie me up,
I'll hold my breath.
If you set me free,
I'll shrivel to death.   (balloon)

Round and full,
Smooth and tight,
Any old color,
Not heavy but light.
Just a tiny hole —
I'll shrink in fright.   *(also a balloon)*

First I'm small,
Then I'm big,
Then I'm small,
Then I'm all gone,
Then I'm small,
Then I'm big,
Then I'm small,
Then I'm all gone.   *(the moon)*

No head but four legs I've got, and a back.
I have my arms, but hands I lack.   *(chair)*

Like a little flame am I,
Mostly pink, and red,
Wiggling, sliding, darting,
In and out your head.   *(tongue)*

I blow smoke through my long mouth.
Hot and hard am I.
Round or square or angle-shaped,
I reach up to the sky.   *(chimney)*

With many little mouths
I speak many sounds,
All along my body,
Long and thin and round.   *(flute)*

Like two little cups
On top of each other,
One is the sister,
And one is the brother.
We make a little house
For someone inside.
With colors and lines
We're covered outside.   *(sea shell, clam)*

I'm a curvy little house
For a tiny little thing.
Though I'm dry when you come in,
You can hear the ocean ring.   *(sea shell)*

Smaller than a loaf of bread,
Bigger than a pin,
I get very soft where
Water hits my skin.
I can help you out
But the more I do,
The smaller I will get,
Until I am through.   *(bar of soap)*

I lie and look at the ceiling,
I'm sure to be quite strong,
But I get stomped and hit and slapped
By everyone who comes along.   *(floor)*

I've got fingers four
But not one more;
I don't have a hand or thumb.
I'm long and skinny;
When you eat your dinny,
I'm waiting there when you come.   *(fork)*

Straight little hair
And a shiny long face,
I'm tall as I can be
With no legs or arms in place.   *(paintbrush)*

You take me in and give me out,
A lot or a little, slow or fast.
Sometimes I let you scream or shout,
Or you hold me tight and make me last.
Yet I'm not to be seen at all, at all,
Whether you look in spring or fall.   *(breath)*

I have long legs and pointed feet,
Get two from one when my legs meet.   *(scissors)*

Like a flattened-out doughnut on the bottom,
Like an upside-down cup on the top,
You can carry me with you everywhere
And I cover up your stringy growing crop.   *(hat)*

Clippers I can cut them with,
Clippers I can grab them,
I don't have any hands at all,
But eight legs to crawl and swim.   *(crab)*

Sometimes I draw straight lines.
Sometimes I draw curved lines.
I always draw on big blue paper.
I use white chalk all the time.
I'm bigger than a house,
But when you see me write,
I look smaller than a mouse.   *(jet airplane)*

I cover up something that's cold and hard
And make it all soft and warm.
But still people step all over me —
Don't they know it does me harm?   (carpet or rug)

I have a long, long nose
And four round feet.
I carry lots of things, including you.
Usually I'm red,
Sometimes I'm ridden.
Whatever is my name?
Let's hear a guess from you.   (child's wagon)

Many little holes in me,
But I don't get wet.
If you put me in the water,
I will float, I bet.   (cork)

Back and forth and forth and back,
Busily we go,
Pushing off the stuff that falls
To let the outside show.   (windshield wipers)

I grow up with my root below.
I grow straight or twist around.
But I have no leaves to show.
I have no flowers to be found.   (hair)

Round and round
I spin and spin.
The more I turn,
The further I'm in.   (screw)

I'm thinner than a leaf.
I can be any color you see.
Round and round I go,
Longer and longer I grow.
Can you guess the name of me?   *(roll of toilet paper)*

Flat round cap, skinny little body,
The sharpest toenail you ever saw.   *(thumbtack)*

Many little black bugs
All on a white sheet
Standing in neat little rows.
If you turn the sheet over,
There's another underneath,
And on and on it goes.   *(book)*

This is mine and mine alone,
But you use it more than I do.   *(my name)*

I'm as light as air,
I'm in every song,
But you can't even hold me
Ten minutes long.   *(breath)*

I have a bright red coat, which is where you start,
But you find many brown children in my heart. *(apple)*

I'm very, very skinny,
But I've got lots of long hair.
I love to stand on my head
And slide everywhere.   *(mop)*

Squeeze some paint on me,
And I'll brush the white fence.
I paint it every day.
Does this make any sense?   *(toothbrush)*

I go up and I go down,
And sometimes I wear a white top.
I don't last long but I come back,
And no one can make me stop.   *(ocean wave)*

I live in the dark
And rarely come out.
I'm long and round
As I dig all about.   *(earthworm)*

Long ago I was a tree,
Standing in the sun.
Now I'm flat as flat can be,
And used by everyone.
I'm white, I'm red, I'm green;
Any color I can be.
And people take their little sticks
And scritch and scratch on me.   *(paper)*

You see me go where you go,
But I never make a sound,
And I disappear when night comes
Or when the sun is not around.   *(shadow)*

Smooth as glass all across,
Bright as a jewel set in white.
When you pull the shade down,
You can say, "Good night."   *(eye)*

I'm a little house
For two long brothers,
But I have no windows,
And I have no doors.
When the two brothers
Want to go in and out,
They lift up the roof
And rise up and out.   *(shoebox)*

You can't hear me talk,
Though you can see me walk.
I walk just like you.
I look just like you.
I move just like you,
But we are two.   *(reflection in mirror or pond)*

More holes than a sponge,
But no one dug them out.
Put me in a trap
To catch a squeaky runabout.
Say my name a while
If you want to smile.   *(cheese)*

I'm one little eye
In a big flat swinger.
You look through me
To see what you can see
After you push the ringer.   *(keyhole)*

All around and around it I ride.
I can be any shape or size.
Many colors I can be.
I just help you to see
What is lying right there inside.   *(picture frame)*

I have two arms;
Back and forth they go.
Though I have four legs,
I haven't got a toe.   *(rocking chair)*

When I wake up from sleep
I'm very, very small.
I grow larger and larger.
I'm not the same at all.
My color even changes,
And then I slump.
I end my life with a
Very long jump.   *(leaf)*

Our house is shiny red on the outside.
Our house is soft and white on the inside.
I and all my brown brothers live in the middle,
And it's a very nice place for us to hide.   *(apple seed)*

Pointed long nose,
Soft round head
(Sometimes two or three).
Put me in the sun,
And just my nose remains.
Any color I can be.   *(ice cream in cone)*

I've got many teeth
To chew through many things.
Back and forth and back and forth.
I'm long and very thin.
You can even make me sing.
Back and forth and back and forth.   *(handsaw)*

I can go round and round in a circle,
Or I go out straight as can be.
If I touch you I like to hold on,
Although you can see through me.   (cellophane/plastic tape)

Back and forth and back and forth.
Two heads have I,
A flat, hard body,
Two long legs
With sharp, pointed toes.
I make one thing
Into two small things
When I go walking
And my legs close.   (scissors)

I have one red tongue
That licks me so slow,
So the older I get,
The smaller I grow.   (candle)

A long, thin neck
With a flat, round head.
You fill me up
When you are fed.   (spoon)

Stories and Story Activities

Most of these tales were originally composed for specific children or classroom situations. Some of them are Waldorf education "pedagogical stories"—that is, stories intended to get across a moral message or inspiration in an indirect way through the imagery called up by the storyteller. Yet it seems to me that each of them could find wider uses than their original purpose. Thus, I present them here, both for others to tell or adapt and as examples of the kinds of stories Waldorf teachers might create for their classes. Although they convey moral lessons, the last two stories with songs include some elements of fantasy probably better suited to the older children in this age range.

The Meeting of the Animals

I have used this story with follow-up classroom activities as a first story of the new school year for a first grade class. It is meant to be adaptable to different situations and groups of children, so feel free to modify some of the details to more closely relate the story to your particular situation. In a simple way, perhaps only with my hand, I act out the movement of each of the animals as I tell the story. The simple line drawings given in the text are a kind of trace of these movements. They also make useful follow-up form drawing exercises and/or group movement activities.

Summer was over and autumn was already ripe. All of the animals in the forest were on the move. The rabbit was hopping:

The snake slithered:

The squirrel eagerly scampered around and around the trees in a winding path:

The nervous chipmunk scooted back and forth as he darted along the forest floor:

The hummingbird flew in a perfectly straight path through the air:

The flock of geese flew in a pattern of straight paths:

The fox moved forward slowly, constantly backtracking his steps:

The raccoon climbed down from a tree, crawled a ways to another tree, went up the tree to look around, and then climbed down again and crawled on further:

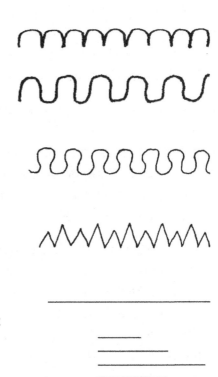

The deer leaped with long, arcing
jumps, moving swiftly along:

The bear lumbered slowly forward
on his heavy feet, one side at a time:

Where were all of the animals going? They were on their way to
the fall meeting they hold every year in the large clearing in the center of
the forest. Here the important decisions for the winter half of the year
must be made. *(The clearing can be described with a few features the children
can identify with their own school or classroom surroundings.)*

One by one, the animals began to arrive in the clearing from many
different directions and regions of the great forest. However, they did not
know that they had brought some secret hitchhikers along with them. As
their furry coats scraped across the plants along their way, they picked
up many tiny seeds and burrs. As the animals arrived in the clearing, they
rubbed off the seeds all around the area.

After the meeting had been held and the animals had enjoyed each
other's company for some time, all the creatures left to go back to their
own homes. Each of them now had a task to carry out for the next half of
the year. The rabbit hopped back through the woods. The snake slithered
off. The squirrel scampered back winding around the trees. The chipmunk
darted back and forth along the ground. The hummingbird flew straight
toward home. The flock of geese flew in their wedge of straight paths. The
fox moved forward and back with his steps. The raccoon climbed down
from a tree, crawled on a bit to another tree, went up the tree to look
around, and so on. The deer leaped swiftly. The bear lumbered away on
his heavy feet.

Time went by and the winter snows fell, covering the forest in a
magic carpet of white. Some animals slept through the winter, and others
huddled in their nests and houses to keep warm and safe. When the first
signs of spring began to appear, the animals started to stir about. Later
in spring it was time for the animals to once again meet together in the

clearing in the center of the forest to make all of the important decisions for the summer half of the year. Each of the animals in its own way began to move toward the forest clearing.

However, a great surprise was waiting for them there. For during the winter all of the seeds and burrs that had fallen from the animals onto the ground in the clearing had grown up into beautiful wildflowers. The entire clearing was filled with the colors of a beautiful bouquet of flowers to welcome the animals back!

In the course of follow-up activities to this story, my first grade class created the "mandala" drawing of the story below. Each radial linear pattern represents the way of moving of one of the animals, and each was drawn in a different color. Of course, a different selection of the animal movement drawings could be made than that used below. The class also learned to recite (and later write) a related verse:

> To the forest meeting the animals came
> Bearing seeds stuck onto their furs.
> Now in spring the clearing is not the same:
> In bright colors it is filled with flowers.

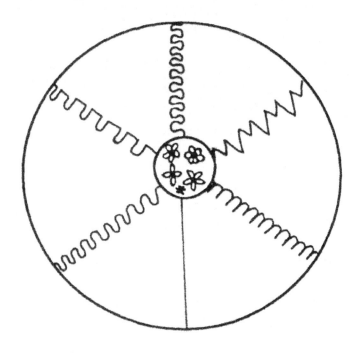

Frosty the Snowflake

Frosty lived on a cold, blue cloud in the vast and airy sky. One day he felt his cousin Wind lifting him up from his cloud home and sending him drifting downward. Soon he found himself sitting comfortably next to many of his white brothers and sisters. He noticed that every one of his six-pointed brothers and sisters was completely different. He felt proud that he was unique, the only one of his kind.

Suddenly, things began to get more crowded. He was pushed up together against his brothers and sisters, as a little boy began to roll him into a snowball. That snowball grew bigger and soon became an ear on the head of a snowman. Now Frosty was high enough to look out far and wide over the whole land. He saw the bare trees, the steam blowing from people's mouths when they breathed or spoke, and the dogs that left their footprints in the snow.

But then he felt the boy lift him up once again, pack him tightly into a snowball, and throw him up onto the roof of a house! Now he could see much farther and higher. He saw the sky, the clouds from which he had come, and the shining sun. He felt the sun most strongly. As the sun slowly sank lower in the sky, it was making him warmer. Frosty felt himself grow softer and softer. He began slowly to slide down the roof.

Just as he had almost reached the edge of the roof, the sun dropped out of sight, and darkness began to creep all around him. He saw the twinkling stars and the moon appear in the sky above. It began to grow cold, and Frosty drifted off to sleep.

When Frosty awoke in the morning light, he found he had become part of a very hard icicle hanging down from the edge of the roof. The morning light shone right through him and made him sparkle. But the sun rose up into the sky again, and the icicle began to melt and drip.

It dripped and dripped, and soon it dripped Frosty right down into a little stream of water that flowed down a hill and into the street. Frosty felt himself rushing down along the street until he ran right down into a drainpipe. The drainpipe deposited him into the great river.

Once in the flowing river, Frosty was no longer so special and unique. He was just one drop in the big river and could hardly tell himself from all of the other drops as they flowed along in one big current.

As he moved along on top of the current, he noticed a large canoe also moving along with the flow. The two men in the canoe dipped their paddles into the water and pushed the boat along, spraying the water from their paddles into the air. Suddenly Frosty felt himself being lifted up on the side of one of the paddles and thrown high into the air.

When he landed, he found himself on a large green leaf growing on one of the trees along the bank of the river. He greeted the leaf politely, but he found himself so tired after his adventures that he soon fell fast asleep on the leaf. While he slept the sun shone warmly on him, and cousin Wind began to blow a bit. Gradually Frosty was caught up into the warm air and lifted gently up toward the sky. (We would say that he was evaporated.)

When he awoke, he was most surprised to find himself back once again on his soft cloud home in the vast and airy sky. It almost seemed as if his adventures as a snowflake and an icicle and a drop had been a long dream, but he knew they hadn't. In fact, he was already looking forward to new adventures soon to come.

After this story, the children sang a short, related song, as follows:

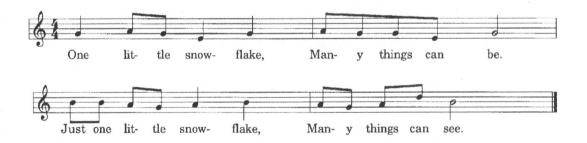

The New Sheep

This animal fable was told to a second grade class who was having difficulty accepting a new student. The "narrow pathway between two groves of trees" was an indirect reference to a hallway the children had difficulty walking down in an orderly way at certain times during the day.

Once there was a flock of sheep who had grazed together ever since they were lambs. They knew all of the best places on their hillside to find greener grass, cool water, and shade in the summer. Every morning and every night (and also at shearing time) when they heard their shepherd ring his bell, they were able to walk along a narrow pathway between two groves of trees that led to the barn where they were fed and spent the night.

One day the shepherd brought a new, black sheep to the flock. He (or she) previously had lived on another farm. Of course, the new sheep was not yet familiar with the daily routine of listening for the shepherd's bell to go back and forth from the pastures to the barn. Nor did he know all of the best places to find green grass, water, and shade. So the other sheep began to make fun of the new sheep when he could not hear them. They laughed at how his wool was trimmed differently than theirs. They felt that they were better and smarter sheep because they knew the best places to graze and drink and rest. So they did not tell these things to the new sheep, who began to feel rather sad and hurt inside.

It happened that wild wolves lived in the forest connected to the grove of trees on the farm. One day the wily creatures learned to make a cry that sounded almost like the shepherd's bell. They hid in the grove of trees near the sheep's pasture and mimicked the sound of the bell. The flock of sheep, not listening too carefully and having the habit of walking to the barn whenever they heard the bell, began walking toward the pathway.

But the new sheep was not fooled, and he noticed that this noise did not sound quite like the real shepherd's bell. He tried to tell some of the other sheep that they should not go to the barn because the bell sounded funny. However, they did not listen because they thought they knew so much more than the new sheep.

As the flock walked between the groves of trees, the wolves leaped out and ate up two of the poor sheep. The others went running back to the pasture as fast as their legs would carry them. After this, the sheep were sorry they had not listened to the new sheep. The new sheep was welcomed into the flock, and everyone shared all they had with him.

The Copper Kingdom

This story activity was inspired by Molly von Heider's eurythmy lesson story "The Water of Life" described in her book Come unto These Yellow Sands *(London: Steiner Schools Fellowship, 1984) and from my experience of her leading such a story-activity during my teacher training. It arose originally around a copper gong and copper bowl that resided in my second grade classroom. Occasional accidents or misbehaviors during the activity could be transformed into additional events in the narrative of the story, if the teacher had enough presence of mind. In this way, the story became always slightly different in action. Both in Molly von Heider's original story, which my class had acted out in first grade, and in "The Copper Kingdom," the attempt was made to have the children engage in certain movements and imaginations that are pedagogically helpful for their age. It was also a lot of fun!*

A word on the drawing at the end, which is intended to be executed in colored crayons: Molly suggested also trying to capture this story (or other stories) in the form of a colored drawing or design, as had been the practice of certain tribal societies (including some Native American tribes) in former times. The drawing captures or summarizes the chief elements of a story in visual patterns and symbols. Here, the copper kingdom lies in the center, surrounded by the weaving path through the forest, with the later events symbolized in order around the outer frame, beginning at the top (e.g., the tiger's stripes, the sand spurs, the bubbling spring).

A line is but a trace of movement, emphasized Rudolf Steiner. Translating the children's story-movement activities into the drawings and symbols of this kind of design reinforces this connection between movement and drawing (also recalling the Form Drawing exercises taught in Waldorf schools). It also repeats the primary generating gesture of writing—the recollection of oral knowledge in meaningful visual forms. In addition, this activity highlights the meaningful movements and hieroglyphic symbolizations behind the written letters of the alphabet, which children of these years are still engaged in mastering. In this way it subtly supports other Waldorf education efforts to teach language as a map of meaningful signs. I have found that such "story-drawings" are well suited to the pictorial form of thought characteristic of children in the first three grades and that such children seem to understand them quite readily.

Once there was a place known as the Copper Kingdom. It was so called because in the center of the kingdom was a great copper castle with four towers and walls that moved each time a great copper bell tolled. *(The children arrange themselves in four rows forming a square. Each time the teacher strikes a bell—or a copper gong—each "wall" of the square castle moves around one place to the right. If desired, an additional step can be added by stating that during the nighttime the walls moved in the reverse direction.)*

The copper castle surrounded and protected the treasure and magic center of the kingdom: a beautiful copper bowl. *(An actual copper bowl—or another, similar vessel—is placed on the floor in the center of the square.)* In the castle lived ___ princes and ___ princesses. *(Use the number of boys and girls in the square.)*

One day, without warning, a giant stomped into the castle. Before anyone knew what was happening, he scooped up the magic copper bowl and strode off with it, saying over his shoulder, "Take back your copper bowl if you can, because I am taking it to my magic castle in the Dark Kingdom." *(The teacher or another adult acts the part of the giant.)*

After the giant left, no one knew what to do. Over the next few days the flowers in the Copper Kingdom began to look less bright, the apples less juicy, the cheeks of the princes and princesses less rosy. Then things all around began to grow old and cracked and withered. Finally, the princes and princesses decided they must go on a journey to the Dark Kingdom to try to recover their magic bowl and save their kingdom.

Since no one had ever been to the Dark Kingdom, they followed the giant's footprints, which they could still see pressed deeply into the ground. This led them through the great forest, as they wound in and out and around, in and out and around. *(Lead the children holding hands in a long row along a continually twisting, turning path.)*

However, the farther they went, the more they began to feel that they weren't really getting anywhere. They were certain they had seen that rotten tree stump before. Surely they had passed that gnarled, old tree less than an hour ago. They realized that the forest must be enchanted, and they decided to get out of the forest by following the sun in a straight line. But even their vision of the sun played tricks on them in the magic wood. They went forward in straight lines, but suddenly it seemed that the sun was in the other direction. As they followed their straight path, they felt themselves going back and forth again over the same territory. *(The children are led in a zig-zag pattern in and out of a circle, gradually progressing around the circle.)*

Suddenly the path they were following ended before a huge cliff, plunging down at their feet. To climb down it, the princes and princesses had to back downward one at a time, clinging to the face of the cliff. They held on tightly to the persons above and behind them for safety as they carefully stepped backward along the crooked path downward. *(The line of children turns, facing the opposite direction. Each child grasps the waist of the child now in front of him or her, and the entire line is led walking backwards along a jagged path. The children should be encouraged not to let go of the person they are facing, lest the whole group fall down the cliff.)*

When the group reached the bottom of the cliff, they found themselves on a broad, open plain where a fierce wind blew them first to the south, then to the north, then to the east, and then to the west. *(In no particular formation the entire group pretends to be blown successively from one side of the room to the other.)*

When the wind died down, the princes and princesses found themselves facing a broad abyss with only a narrow bridge of a single log to lead them across. *(This could be a balance beam.)* When the first ones tried to cross the bridge, they soon discovered it was enchanted. It had the strange characteristic that, when half of the group had crossed over the bridge, the first person of the other half of the group could get across only if one of the first half crossed back over again at the same time. So two by two the princes and princesses tried to cross the narrow bridge together without falling off into the deep chasm below. *(This activity is just as described. The children must devise workable strategies so that two persons can cross at the same time from opposite ends of the balance beam. If anyone falls off the beam, they must sit out until they can perhaps be rescued or disenchanted later in the story.)*

Once the group had crossed the chasm, they found themselves facing a narrow passageway of sand between two tall rock cliffs. In the sand were growing prickly sandspurs that no one wanted to step on. But worse still, a fierce tiger lay sleeping just by the entrance to the sandy passageway. One by one, the princes and princesses crept up to the passageway and tried to scamper across it without being caught by the tiger or stepping on the sandspurs. *(The narrow passageway can be defined by two long lines on either side [rope, rods, balance beams, etc.]. The sandspurs can be bean bags scattered around the passageway. Those who step on one must hop on one leg for the rest of the journey. The teacher or adult can play the role of the tiger. Children caught by the tiger are taken off to the tiger's den—perhaps a corner of the room—where they must wait until they can perhaps be rescued later in the story.)*

Those who passed safely through the narrow passageway continued around the edge of a rocky cliffside. On their right in a niche in the rock, they soon saw a bubbling spring. Those who were weary or injured found themselves refreshed or healed if they drank or bathed in the water of that spring *(a useful cure for those lamed by the sandspurs).*

As they rounded another bend, the view opened up before their eyes. They saw a huge castle looming a short distance before them. It seemed to be carved out of the dark-colored rock of the cliffside, and they did not doubt that they had finally found the giant's home in the Dark Kingdom.

As they peered from behind a row of bushes, they noticed two large, gated entrances to the castle grounds. The gate of the first was open, but it was guarded by a large armed man. The gate of the second was closed, but there was enough room under the bottom of the gate for the princes and princesses to crawl through beneath it. They decided to send out one of the princesses to distract the guard, while the rest would crawl in under the closed gate.

The princess walked up to the guard and pretended to be lost and hungry, asking for something to eat. While she talked with the guard, the rest crawled under the other gate one by one. *(The closed gate might be a desk or another suitable space to crawl through or under.)*

They found themselves in front of a small door in the side of the castle. Entering, they noticed they were in the kitchen. Suddenly they spotted a small mouse moving along the back wall. They asked him where they could find the giant, and the mouse told them where the giant slept, guarding the stolen copper bowl, which was now filled with a magic but poisonous liquid that held the power of the giant's spell over the castle.

The mouse warned them that the giant's room could be entered only by walking backwards and that they must repeat softly, "Sleep, giant, sleep" as they climbed the ladder to reach the copper bowl resting on the giant's bedside table. If the giant awakened, he would turn any intruders into stone. Should they obtain the bowl, continued the mouse, they must pour its contents into the bottomless well at the other end of the room. Then all would be well at last.

Holding hands, the princes and princesses walked backwards into a spiral and back out again to enter the giant's room. One by one they attempted to scale the ladder and rescue the copper bowl. (*The children hold hands and the leader guides them to walk along a spiral pathway. Upon reaching center of the spiral, the line turns and passes back out of the spiral along the same path. When the children emerge from the spiral, their backs will face the center of the circle. They must again go back in and out of the spiral to be facing the center of the circle. The ladder can be formed of several copper rods laid in a row several inches apart and leading up to the water-filled copper bowl on a small table or desk. As each child moves forward to climb the ladder, the sleeping giant, played by the teacher or an adult, snores three times before waking up. If the child steps on one of the copper rods, this also wakes the giant. The aroused giant turns the child to stone by pointing a finger. Once a child has picked up the bowl, the giant cannot wake up. I recommend limiting these attempts to three children per story. If one is successful, the story continues to its conclusion, as below. If no one is successful, the story ends with the giant victorious.*)

As soon as the magic, poisonous liquid was poured into the bottomless well, the magic spell the giant had cast on the castle was broken. All of the people of the castle, who had been turned into animals or other forms (except the guard by the gate), were changed back to their true forms in an instant. The castle was changed from dark rock to shining white marble. The mouse turned back into the king of the castle and immediately told the guard at the gate to go back home and let the princes and princesses pass out freely.

After thanking the king for his help, the princes and princesses walked back over the path they had taken to come to the Dark Kingdom. Now, however, they met nothing enchanted or threatening, for the giant's evil spell had been broken. *(Children walk back along the cliffside and through*

Diagrammatic Drawing for the Copper Kingdom

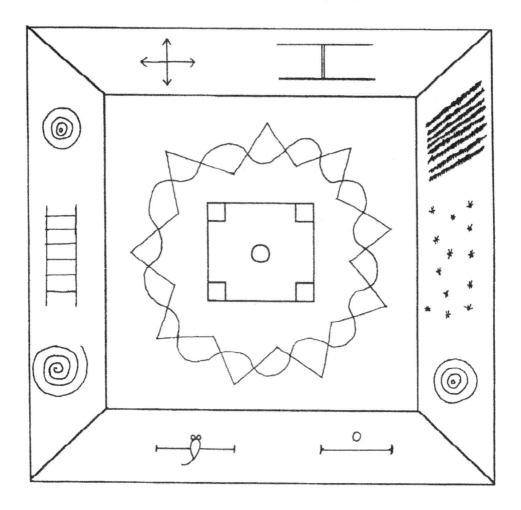

the narrow passageway [where the sandspurs have lost their power to wound],
where they meet the tiger who has been changed back into his true form of a
wizard. He gives back anyone who has been taken to the tiger's den, and the
children continue across the now normal narrow bridge over the chasm, across
the broad, open plain [now windless], back up the path leading up the cliff, and
straight through the once enchanted forest.)

Arriving back in the Copper Kingdom, they restored the bowl to its place of honor in the center of the castle. Once again the flowers of the Copper Kingdom grew brightly colored, the apples ripe and juicy, and the cheeks of the princes and princesses a rosy red. Once again the four straight castle walls moved around the corner towers each time the copper gong (or bell) sounded. Once again all was good and healthy in the Copper Kingdom.

The Caterpillar and the Elf

"Inch up! Inch up! Inch up!" That is how the small caterpillar slowly moves up the branch of the cherry tree he is climbing, bending his long, round body and moving each pair of his many legs one after the other. But suddenly both the caterpillar and the branch start to shake and shake. The caterpillar is trembling because he is afraid, and he is making the entire branch shake.

All of this shaking soon wakes up a wee elf, who has been sleeping in a nearby cherry blossom. "What is all this commotion about?" he calls out. But the caterpillar is too afraid to even talk. He just goes on shaking and points upward with one little leg. Looking above, the elf sees the dark shadow of a large crow circling the cherry tree, looking for something to eat and coming ever closer to the caterpillar. "Oh, now I see why you are trembling so much in fear," exclaims the elf.

Mustering up his courage, the caterpillar manages to speak to the elf: "Oh, please, Mr. Elf, if you will just save me from that crow, I will surely repay the favor by helping you sometime." The elf thinks it quite amusing that a mere caterpillar who crawls around all day could do anything to help an unusual fellow such as himself. Because the very idea makes him laugh, he agrees to help the poor caterpillar. Taking out the magic wand he keeps in his back pocket, he twirls it through the air, magically making the cherry tree seem a very unpleasant place for the crow. The crow soon flew away.

"Thank you from the bottom of my heart," says the caterpillar. "You will see that I will help you someday as well." Chuckling to himself over this notion, the elf climbs back into his cherry blossom to continue his nap.

Time goes by, and the cherry blossoms turn into cherries. The cherries fall from the tree. Then the leaves turn brown and also begin to fall from the tree. The caterpillar curls up inside one of these leaves within a soft, warm bed he made for himself. Soon he is fast asleep. In fact, he sleeps so soundly, he does not even notice when that leaf too sails down from the cherry tree and lands in some plants on the ground below. Soon it is covered with winter snow, but the caterpillar sleeps on soundly.

Now, picture the sun shining brightly with many-colored spring flowers blooming all across a wide meadow. Picture Mr. Elf striding across that meadow feeling free and carefree. But notice that Dragonfly comes buzzing in from across the field. Dragonfly is a mischievous trickster and often does not play very nice tricks. He can fly very fast and quietly, and that is how he darts up toward Mr. Elf. He sees the end of Mr. Elf's magic wand sticking out of his pocket and swoops down, grabbing the wand. As he flies off into the air, Mr. Elf spots him and grows furious. He shouts and screams at Dragonfly and hops up and down, but Dragonfly just laughs and flies off with the wand. Mr. Elf makes such a racket that he wakes up someone who has been sleeping all winter long.

Curled up inside of a nearby leaf is Caterpillar. But when Caterpillar climbs out of his winter bed, he finds he has changed. He has been transformed into a butterfly, with broad and beautiful colored wings. He notices the elf shouting and hopping and calls out to him, "Mr. Elf! Maybe I can help you. After all, you helped me once."

"That Dragonfly has stolen my magic wand!" yells the angry elf. "Now I cannot work any more of my magic to help Mother Nature."

"Then climb onto my back, and we can fly after Dragonfly and try to get back your wand," replies the butterfly.

The elf at first can hardly believe that this was the sluggish caterpillar he had seen on the cherry tree last summer, but he climbs onto the back of the butterfly and off they fly. Slowly they fly closer and closer behind the dragonfly. As he rides along on the back of the butterfly, the elf sings a little song, which goes like this:

Butterfly Rider

1. I can fly 'cross the sky On my but-ter-fly steed,
2. I fly past Broth-er Wind On my but-ter-fly steed,

Ride through the clouds Till the drag-on-fly we see.
Through Sis-ter Mist Till the drag-on-fly we see.

Drag-on-fly! Drag-on-fly! We will find you soon.
Drag-on-fly! Drag-on-fly! We will find you soon.

Soon the elf and the butterfly grow close enough to the dragonfly to see him carrying the elf's wand in his mouth as he flies along. The butterfly flies high above the dragonfly and then swoops right down at him. He flies close enough to Dragonfly that Mr. Elf is able to reach out and snatch back his magic wand from Dragonfly's mouth. He then stands up on the butterfly's back and speaks to Dragonfly.

"Dragonfly, you have wings to fly with, but you do not use them for good but only to play evil tricks on others. Therefore, I use my wand to turn you into a toad that will never fly again but will have to hop about on the ground to find your food."

Instantly the dragonfly is turned into a toad and has to spend many years as a toad to learn the value of having wings. But the elf and the butterfly remained the best of friends, and sometimes that summer they would find themselves singing together the elf's chase song.

The Redbird and the Crystal Mountain

Once there lived a young girl whose name was Helen. One day she decided to leave her home and go on a journey through the forest. Fearlessly she set off, walking along the forest path.

Suddenly, without so much as a rumble of thunder or a flash of lightning for a warning, it began to rain. The rain poured down, and Helen was getting very wet—until she found a large hollow tree, inside of which she could take refuge from the angry rainstorm.

Just as she was feeling safe and cozy inside of the hollow tree, she was startled to hear a cracked, wee voice behind her speak out, "And who might you be who come right into a person's home without an invitation?"

The surprised girl turned her head around and found herself looking straight at a small, old elf who had made his home inside this hollow tree. Very politely Helen answered, "I am Helen. I am very sorry to have intruded, Sir Elf. I was just beginning a long journey through the forest when it began to rain, so I came in here for shelter. I did not know it was your home. I will quickly go out again if I have offended you."

The elf was pleased with this courteous reply and told the girl, "No, you do not need to go. You are welcome to stay here until the rain stops. But let me tell you something: This is a very dangerous forest for a little girl to go walking through. In this forest is a wolf, a fierce wolf who eats people!"

"He wouldn't eat me," said Helen, although she didn't quite know what she would do if she were to meet a wolf.

The elf said to her, "No, the wolf will not eat you if you will listen to my advice. I will give you a very special red berry. If you ever meet the wolf, then you must quickly swallow the berry, and he will not be able to catch you. That is the only way I know to escape the wolf. I hope it will help you."

Helen thanked the old elf for his kind gift. Noticing that the rain had stopped falling, she said good-bye to the elf and continued on her journey through the forest. The deeper she walked into the wood, the darker it grew. But she was not afraid, and she carried the red berry in a safe place in the very bottom of her pocket.

Later in the day, just as Helen was beginning to grow tired from so much walking, she heard a sound behind her. Turning about, she was frightened to see the big, dark wolf standing right in the path, looking straight at her with a hungry gleam in his eye. She could see the white glow of his long, sharp teeth as he began to walk toward her.

Then Helen said, "You aren't going to eat me, Mr. Wolf." She took her red berry out of her pocket and quickly swallowed it. Instantly she was changed into a redbird! She flew up into a tree where the wolf could not reach her, and he had to go away.

Helen was glad to have escaped from the evil wolf, but she was very surprised and alarmed to be turned into a bird. She did not know how to regain her rightful form.

She decided to ask the other birds in the forest for help. First of all, she went to the blue jay. The blue jay was proudly chattering at some small sparrows, explaining all the ways he was so much bigger and better than they were. When the redbird Helen asked the blue jay for help, he pretended that he could not be bothered with such little problems, though he really did not know how to help her.

After this, she went to ask the crow for help, but the crow would only caw very loudly at her and ask her to agree that he was a very beautiful bird (which really he was not).

Then she went to the woodpecker. He was busy tapping industriously on a tree with his long, sharp bill. When he heard the redbird's problem, he advised her to fly to the high mountain crag where the wise eagle lived and ask him what to do. Helen thanked the woodpecker and flew up to see the wise eagle on his crag.

When the eagle heard her story, he thought for a long while, and then he told her, "There is only one way I know by which you may come to walk on earth again. To the east of this forest near the foot of the great mountain, there lives in a little hut a hermit, a wise old man who speaks the language of the birds and beasts. Perhaps in his wisdom he may know of something you can do to regain your rightful form. Many times has he helped us bird folk. Go to him and he may help you also."

Helen thanked the wise eagle for his sage advice and flew off toward the east in search of the hermit's little hut. She had flown nearly to the great mountain when she spied a small house of logs with a grass roof. As she flew closer to it, a cheerful man with a yellow cap and a long beard appeared at the door, speaking to her in the speech of the redbirds, "Welcome! Welcome, Helen. I have been expecting you to come. Come sit here and let us talk."

"You were expecting me?" asked Helen in disbelief. "How do you know my name?"

"Oh, I know your name and a great deal more besides," answered the hermit. "But all in good time. Will you have some raspberries to eat with me? They are very sweet and juicy."

Helen said that she would like some raspberries, and the two of them fell to eating. The berries were a rich red and even tastier than the hermit had said. But all this while Helen grew more and more impatient to tell the hermit why she had flown to seek him. Finally, she burst out speaking, telling the good old man of her problem and asking if he knew a way for her to walk on earth again.

The hermit scratched his beard and spoke, "I see you cannot wait, and it is good that you are so eager to solve your problem. But eagerness and good will must always make friends with wisdom. When you left your home to journey through the forest, you did not think enough about the dangers. The wolf will try to eat all those who walk through his forest unprepared. You must earn for yourself a protection from the wolf before you may continue your journey in your rightful form.

"I will tell you just what you must do. You first must fly up to the very top of this great mountain. It is a long, hard flight with strong winds and sharp rocks hidden by clouds to get in your way. At the very top, you will find a small bed of shining crystals, which will seem to you as if the very stars had caught themselves upon the mountain top. You must take a crystal in your beak and walk all the way back down the mountain. If it drops from your beak before you reach the mountain's bottom, all will be lost. If you carry out this task well, then you yourself will see what good it may do, and you will be able to continue safely on your journey through the wood."

In this way the wise, old longbeard spoke. Thinking over every word the kindly hermit had said, Helen thanked him again and again and said her farewell. "God help you in your tasks," the hermit called out to her as she flew toward the great mountain.

Slowly and surely the redbird began flying up toward the distant top of the mountain, which she could not see, buried, as it was, in the clouds. Fierce winds began to blow and buffet her about, but still she kept pushing on. Helen found that she must keep a keen watch for the sharp rocks hidden in the foggy, mountain air.

In this way a very tired redbird managed to make it to the tip-top of the mountain. Coming to a rest, she was dazzled by the sparkling bed of crystals. It seemed to her a beautiful, heavenly sight, and she hardly dared to pluck one up, any more than she would try to pluck a star out of the nighttime sky.

Gathering up her courage, the redbird picked up one of the shining crystals in her beak. Turning around, she began the long walk back down the mountain. As she walked on and on, the day grew older and the sun began to set. The red and orange sky glowed and sparkled in the crystal held tightly in her beak. Soon it was dark all around her, and she had only the moon and stars to light her way. Still she walked on, and as she came nearer and nearer to the bottom of the mountain, she felt as if she were growing longer and longer. But she could not see well enough to tell what was happening.

She was just nearing the bottom of the mountain when the first faint glow of the dawn lit up the hills in the distance. As she set her feet on flat ground once again, the sun just peeked over the hills, and she could see what had happened to her. Helen had turned back into a girl again— and her crystal had turned into a gleaming silver sword!

When she saw the wonderful thing that had happened to her, she wished a prayer of thanksgiving in her heart for the kind and wise hermit on the other side of the mountain. Then, taking up her sword in her right hand, Helen walked on into the forest to continue her journey. After a while the wolf heard her coming, but when he saw her shining silver sword, he was afraid and would not come too near her.

In this way Helen walked fearlessly on through the great forest, searching for her destiny. As she walked, she often sang this little song:

The wolf, the wolf I do not fear,
For he is there and I am here. I
walk the earth be- neath the sky, Though once as
bird I had to fly. My sword is shin- ing
bright and true, When I am kind in all I do.

Songs

Many of these songs reflect Rudolf Steiner's recommendation to sing "in the mood of the fifth" with young children (which I interpret as referring to children of ages eight or nine years and younger). The interval of the fifth has a quality of wide, impersonal openness, something like a first grader's wide-eyed openness and sense of oneness with the surrounding world.

Nearly all of these songs are also composed within a particular pentatonic scale. Beginning with an A above middle C, approximately in the center of a child's vocal range, we can range a fifth above to E and a fifth below to D. This defines the average comfortable singing range for most younger children. Within this range, still centered on the A, we construct a pentatonic scale with no half tones—that is, we omit the F and C to give the descending sequence: E D B A G E D. This scale provides another open-sounding, softer structure upon which we may weave children's melodies. Songs can range adventurously out toward the peripheries of this scale or find their way back "home" toward the A, with many variations and side journeys in between. This contrasts with our typical adult, earthbound music that insists on resolving melodies back to a tonic. Having said this, I hasten to add that not every one of the songs included here completely achieves this free-floating quality.

Music is always in motion, and Steiner, in fact, points to the movement of the interval as the essential element of music. The interval is that which we do not hear in the motion "between" the sounding tones, and each interval has its own individual quality. This flow of movement from one tone to the next is melody, and all but one of the songs included here are unharmonized melodies.

An emphasis on the element of movement can be brought into singing most effectively with children in grades one to three if it is done in a pictorial, imaginative fashion. I suggest two ways to accomplish this. The imaginative element can be "built in" through the way movement patterns of the melody reflect and relate to the song's content. Many of these songs attempt to do this.

In addition, the adult can have the children make movements (primarily arm and hand movements) that meaningfully accompany the songs, either flowing with the melody or in some way pictorializing the song content. If the adult repeatedly carries out these movements before the children while singing, most children will naturally imitate them, either sooner or later. Even those who only observe the adult's movements are experiencing through their senses something of this enhanced quality of musical movement. It is out of early childhood limb movements that speech first condenses. Giving children a chance to move in connection with singing reinforces this relationship, maintaining it and letting it gradually, naturally fade into the background toward the third grade.

The ultimate, most deeply grounded experience of movement in relation to speech and song is to be found in the new art of pedagogical eurythmy, as it was founded by Steiner and is typically taught in the Waldorf schools by trained eurythmists. Some suggestions for movements that I have used with children are given for many of the songs included here, but please feel encouraged to create your own movements.

I should also include a word about the endings of songs. A few of the songs provide two different final notes as two possible or optional endings. As young children are still involved in a process of "waking up" or "coming down" to the surrounding physical world, their music can support this by not overemphasizing a grounding in a strong bass beat or by not emphasizing the end of the song as a "return" or "landing" back on the physical "ground note" of the scale.

One of my teachers, Elisabeth Lebret, used to say that we use singing to try to lower the children gently down on a parachute during these years, and this is a reason also for using the "mood of the fifth" and a "centered" pentatonic scale (rather than a scale grounded in a tonic). It better harmonizes with this "floating," dreamy consciousness of young children if the final note does not imply a "grounding" or conclusion of a musical cadence, but is rather left hovering or rising. As children get closer to third grade, this becomes less important.

Thus, two choices are given for some final notes, depending on the maturity of the children involved. A few songs also end with some kind of surprise, often a sudden clap. When children become a bit familiar with the surprise ending, it will increase their participation and enjoyment in singing the song if they come to anticipate the ending, or, perhaps, wonder if their classmates will remember to perform the surprise.

Finally, I should caution against too strict an interpretation of the meter in these songs. Guidance should certainly be given by the adult's singing, but the actual "time signature" should arise out of the natural singing activity of the children.

Several of the songs included here are either collaborative efforts with other teachers or include lyrics that were written by someone else. If no alternative author or composer is listed, the song was created by me.

Stream, Stream

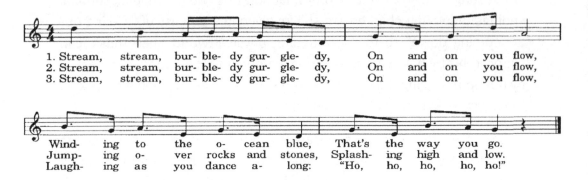

1. Stream, stream, bur-ble-dy gur-gle-dy, On and on you flow,
2. Stream, stream, bur-ble-dy gur-gle-dy, On and on you flow,
3. Stream, stream, bur-ble-dy gur-gle-dy, On and on you flow,

Wind-ing to the o-cean blue, That's the way you go.
Jump-ing o-ver rocks and stones, Splash-ing high and low.
Laugh-ing as you dance a-long: "Ho, ho, ho, ho, ho!"

Falling Leaves

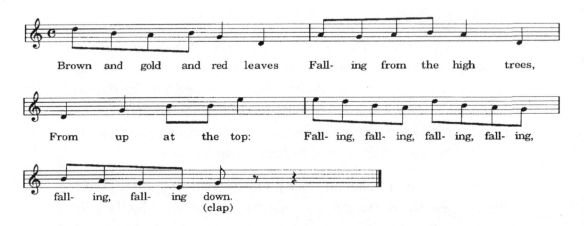

Brown and gold and red leaves Fall-ing from the high trees,

From up at the top: Fall-ing, fall-ing, fall-ing, fall-ing,

fall-ing, fall-ing down.
(clap)

In both of these songs the shape and flow of the melody line imitates that of the natural activity being described. Both songs come alive more readily when accompanied by arm movements. When singing "Falling Leaves" with children, I recommend "climbing" stepwise in the air with both hands during the third measure and then descending with the hands during the fourth and fifth measures while swaying the hands gently from side to side. Try to "surprise" the children with the final clap.

Sing Cricket, Sing

Sing, crick- et, sing, sing, Sing, crick- et, sing. All night long your
mu- sic rings. Chir- rup chir- rup chee chee, Chir- rup chir- rup chee.
Chir- rup chir- rup chee chee Chir- rup chir- rup chee. Sing, cricket, sing, sing,
Sing, cricket, sing. To our ears your sweet sounds bring.

This song is much enhanced if one can introduce a rhythm instrument or two to mimic cricket sounds. My standard practice is to pass out two differently pitched guiros (ideally to children seated in opposite ends of the room) and have them stroke alternately on each beat during the "Chirrup chirrup chee" section. But please experiment with your own cricket chirps!

Freckled Fish

Lyrics, author unknown

Melody, David Adams

Freck- led fish- es flirt- ing, flit- ting, Flash- ing fast and float- ing free,
Flick- ing fil- my fins like feath- ers, Feed- ing from the flow- ing sea.

59

Little Dewdrops

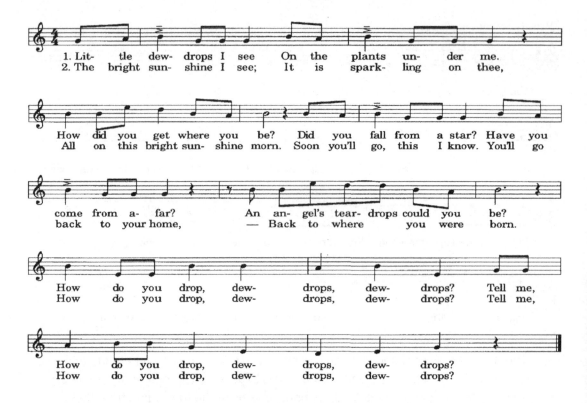

1. Lit- tle dew- drops I see On the plants un- der me.
2. The bright sun- shine I see; It is spark- ling on thee,

How did you get where you be? Did you fall from a star? Have you
All on this bright sun- shine morn. Soon you'll go, this I know. You'll go

come from a- far? An an- gel's tear- drops could you be?
back to your home, — Back to where you were born.

How do you drop, dew- drops, dew- drops? Tell me,
How do you drop, dew- drops, dew- drops? Tell me,

How do you drop, dew- drops, dew- drops?
How do you drop, dew- drops, dew- drops?

Suggestion: A triangle struck lightly on the first beat of each measure adds a nice touch to this song.

Le Ciel Est Bleu

Lyrics, Michael Nettleton

Melody, David Adams

Le ciel est bleu. Je suis heu- reux, Et

dans mon âme Je suis calm.

Translation: The sky is blue, I am happy, And in my soul I am calm.

Where Go the Boats?

Lyrics, Robert Louis Stevenson

Melody, David Adams

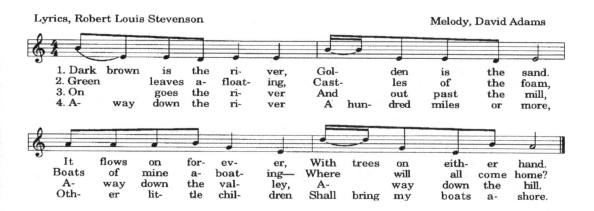

1. Dark brown is the ri- ver, Gol- den is the sand.
2. Green leaves a- float- ing, Cast- les of the foam,
3. On goes the ri- ver And out past the mill,
4. A- way down the ri- ver A hun- dred miles or more,

It flows on for- ev- er, With trees on eith- er hand.
Boats of mine a- boat- ing— Where will all come home?
A- way down the val- ley, A- way down the hill.
Oth- er lit- tle chil- dren Shall bring my boats a- shore.

I'd Like to Be a Worm

Lyrics, author unknown

Melody, David Adams

I'd like to be a worm And squirm in nice soft

dirt And not have to wor- ry or ev- er be

sor- ry Of get- ting mud on my nice clean

shirt.

The Squirrel

Lyrics, author unknown

Melody, David Adams

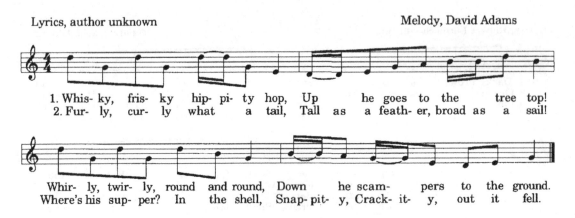

1. Whis- ky, fris- ky hip- pi- ty hop, Up he goes to the tree top!
2. Fur- ly, cur- ly what a tail, Tall as a feath- er, broad as a sail!

Whir- ly, twir- ly, round and round, Down he scam- pers to the ground.
Where's his sup- per? In the shell, Snap- pit- y, Crack- it- y, out it fell.

Good Morning

Lyrics, Muriel Sipe

Melody, David Adams

1. One day I saw a down- y duck With feath- ers on his back; I
2. One day I saw a tim- id mouse, He was so shy and meek; I
3. One day I saw a cur- ly dog, I met him with a bow; I
4. One day I saw a scar- let bird, He woke me from my sleep; I

said, "Good morn- ing, down- y duck." And he said, "Quack, quack, quack."
said, "Good morn- ing, tim- id mouse." And he said, "Squeak, squeak, squeak."
said, "Good morn- ing, cur- ly dog." And he said, "Bow - wow- wow."
said, "Good morn- ing, scar- let bird." And he said, "Cheep, cheep, cheep."

An extra element of interest can be added to this song my making the children guess the sound made by each animal at the end. The adult stops singing on "And he said," and the children (or perhaps an individual child chosen by the adult) must correctly complete the line. I encourage you to make up additional verses about other animals. For example: "One day I saw a spotted frog. In the water for a soak..." You can guess the ending.

Little Snowflake

Translated German Folk Song, from
Sing through the Seasons

Melody, David Adams

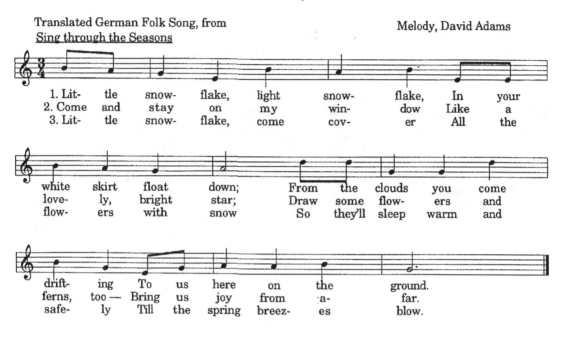

1. Lit- tle snow- flake, light snow- flake, In your
2. Come and stay on my win- dow Like a
3. Lit- tle snow- flake, come cov- er All the

white skirt float down; From the clouds you come
love- ly, bright star; Draw some flow- ers and
flow- ers with snow So they'll sleep warm and

drift- ing To us here on the ground.
ferns, too — Bring us joy from a- far.
safe- ly Till the spring breez- es blow.

Tumbleweed

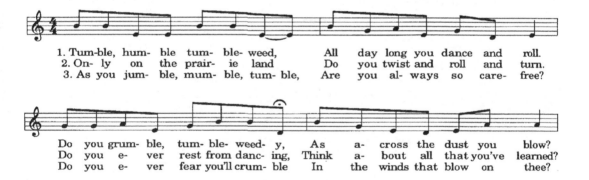

1. Tum- ble, hum- ble tum- ble- weed, All day long you dance and roll.
2. On- ly on the prair- ie land Do you twist and roll and turn.
3. As you jum- ble, mum- ble, tum- ble, Are you al- ways so care- free?

Do you grum- ble, tum- ble- weed- y, As a- cross the dust you blow?
Do you e- ver rest from danc- ing, Think a- bout all that you've learned?
Do you e- ver fear you'll crum- ble In the winds that blow on thee?

Both of these songs feature melody lines whose movement imitates their subject. Find your own arm movements to echo their melodic paths. I recommend trying "Tumbleweed" with the following ostinato, perhaps played on a small xylophone or glockenspiel.

Snow

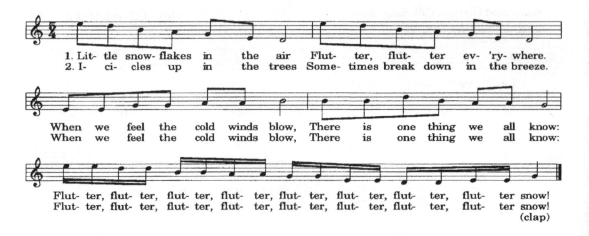

1. Lit- tle snow- flakes in the air Flut- ter, flut- ter ev- 'ry- where.
2. I- ci- cles up in the trees Some- times break down in the breeze.

When we feel the cold winds blow, There is one thing we all know:
When we feel the cold winds blow, There is one thing we all know:

Flut- ter, flut- ter, flut- ter, flut- ter, flut- ter, flut- ter, flut- ter, flut- ter snow!
Flut- ter, flut- ter, flut- ter, flut- ter, flut- ter, flut- ter, flut- ter, flut- ter snow!
(clap)

Skating

Lyrics, Jane Wulsin and David Adams

Melody, David Adams and Jane Wulsin

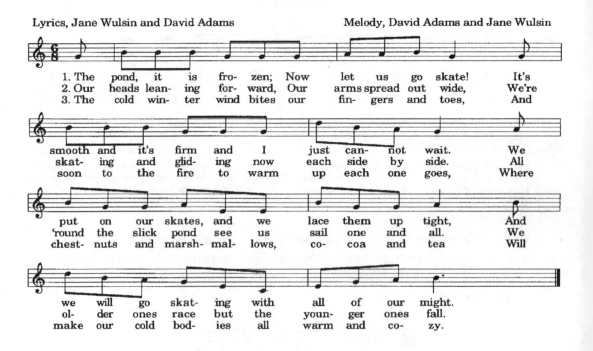

1. The pond, it is fro- zen; Now let us go skate! It's
2. Our heads lean- ing for- ward, Our arms spread out wide, We're
3. The cold win- ter wind bites our fin- gers and toes, And

smooth and it's firm and I just can- not wait. We
skat- ing and glid- ing now each side by side. All
soon to the fire to warm up each one goes, Where

put on our skates, and we lace them up tight, And
'round the slick pond see us sail one and all. We
chest- nuts and marsh- mal- lows, co- coa and tea Will

we will go skat- ing with all of our might.
ol- der ones race but the youn- ger ones fall.
make our cold bod- ies all warm and co- zy.

Epiphany Song

Lyrics, Heiner and Marianne Garff
Translated by David and Janet Adams

Melody, adapted by David Adams
from Heiner and Marianne Garff

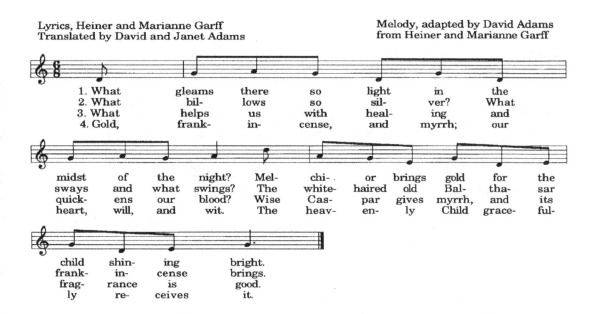

1. What gleams there so light in the midst of the night? Mel- chi- or brings gold for the child shin- ing bright.
2. What bil- lows so sil- ver? What sways and what swings? The white- haired old Bal- tha- sar frank- in- cense brings.
3. What helps us with heal- ing and quick- ens our blood? Wise Cas- par gives myrrh, and its frag- rance is good.
4. Gold, frank- in- cense, and myrrh; our heart, will, and wit. The heav- en- ly Child grace- ful- ly re- ceives it.

Ice

Lyrics, adapted from
Dorothy Aldis

Melody, David Adams

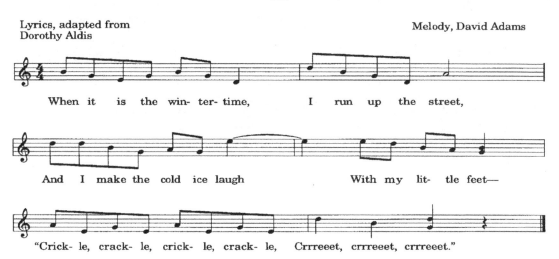

When it is the win- ter- time, I run up the street,

And I make the cold ice laugh With my lit- tle feet—

"Crick- le, crack- le, crick- le, crack- le, Crrreeet, crrreeet, crrreeet."

65

White Fields

Lyrics, James Stephens

Melody, David Adams

In the win- ter time we go Walk- ing in the
fields of snow; Where there is no grass at all;
Where the top of ev- 'ry wall, Ev- 'ry fence, and
ev- 'ry tree, Is as white as white can be.
Point- ing out the way we came, — Ev- 'ry one of
them the same — All a- cross the fields there be
Prints in sil- ver fil- i- gree; And our moth- ers
al- ways know, By the foot- prints in the snow,
Where it is we chil- dren go.

Lemon Song

Lyrics, Martin Schmandt

Melody, David Adams

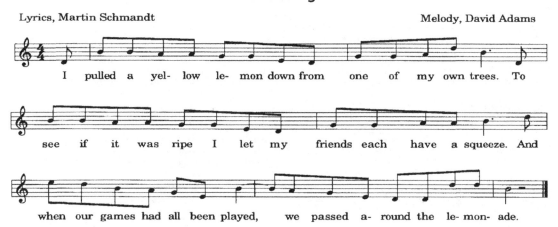

I pulled a yel- low le- mon down from one of my own trees. To
see if it was ripe I let my friends each have a squeeze. And
when our games had all been played, we passed a- round the le- mon- ade.

This song is a circle game I have adapted from Martin Schmandt, a former
Waldorf teacher in Applegate, California. As I play it, the game begins with the
adult reaching up and pulling down an imaginary lemon as the song begins. This
is passed around by the adult squeezing the land of a child next to him. This
child passes the "lemon squeeze" on to the next child, and so on around the
circle. Whoever is receiving the squeeze when the song ends get to "drink" the
lemonade.

Animals' Lullaby

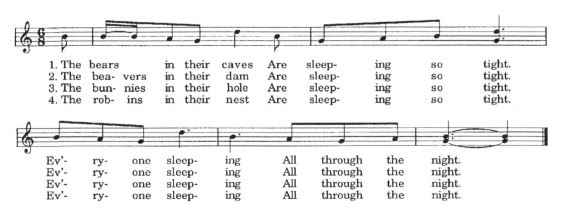

1. The bears in their caves Are sleep- ing so tight.
2. The bea- vers in their dam Are sleep- ing so tight.
3. The bun- nies in their hole Are sleep- ing so tight.
4. The rob- ins in their nest Are sleep- ing so tight.

Ev'- ry- one sleep- ing All through the night.
Ev'- ry- one sleep- ing All through the night.
Ev'- ry- one sleep- ing All through the night.
Ev'- ry- one sleep- ing All through the night.

This song is intended to be a practical lullaby, with the singer continuing to make
up verses until the child falls asleep. The four verses here are just examples.
Insects, amphibians, reptiles and all wild and tame creatures can be brought into
the song as needed (or perhaps as requested).

Springtime

1. The lark is sing- ing, The flow- ers are ring- ing, The
2. The snail is creep- ing, The chicks are peep- ing, The
3. The frogs are jump- ing, The rab- bits are thump- ing, The

hare is spring- ing, High and low,
deer are leap- ing, High and low,
hors- es are clump- ing, High and low,

High and low. Spring- time, spring- time, all a- glow.
High and low. Spring- time, spring- time, all a- glow.
High and low. Spring- time, spring- time, all a- glow.

Call to Spring

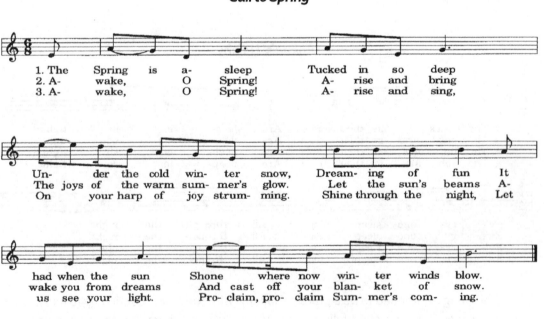

1. The Spring is a- sleep Tucked in so deep
2. A- wake, O Spring! A- rise and bring
3. A- wake, O Spring! A- rise and sing,

Un- der the cold win- ter snow, Dream- ing of fun It
The joys of the warm sum- mer's glow. Let the sun's beams A-
On your harp of joy strum- ming. Shine through the night, Let

had when the sun Shone where now win- ter winds blow.
wake you from dreams And cast off your blan- ket of snow.
us see your light. Pro- claim, pro- claim Sum- mer's com- ing.

Pitter Patter Pit

Lyrics, Alan Hirsch

Melody, Alan Hirsch

This is one of several songs written by or co-written with Alan Hirsch, who was my teaching colleague in Denver in 1973-1974. I often emphasize the raindrop rhythm by having the singing children either step to the beat walking around a circle or else tap to the beat with two fingers on the palm of the hand (or, with caution, tap with their little fingers on their desks). They steps or beats continue to be heard on the rests. Another way to enhance the song is to have one child play the first "pitter patter pit" phrase as a repeated ostinato on a xylophone or similar instrument (with the G on "pit" held as a half note).

Ladybug

Lyrics, Traditional

Melody, David Adams

La- dy- bug, La- dy- bug, Fly a- way home!

Your house is on fire And your chil- dren might burn.

Little Charlie

Lyrics, Helen Cowles LeCror

Melody, David Adams

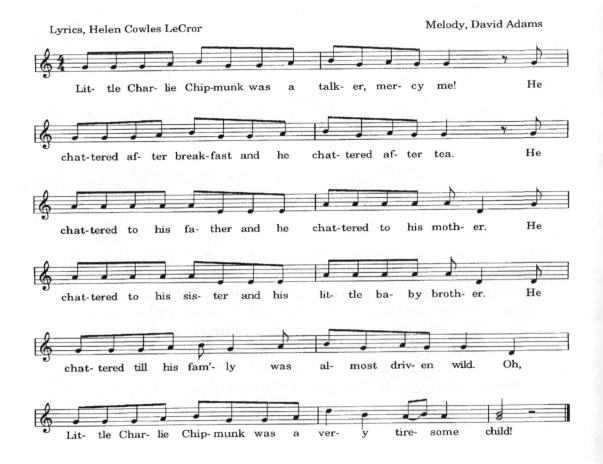

Lit- tle Char- lie Chip-munk was a talk- er, mer- cy me! He

chat-tered af- ter break-fast and he chat- tered af- ter tea. He

chat-tered to his fa- ther and he chat-tered to his moth- er. He

chat-tered to his sis- ter and his lit- tle ba- by broth- er. He

chat- tered till his fam'- ly was al- most driv- en wild. Oh,

Lit- tle Char- lie Chip- munk was a ver- y tire- some child!

A Little Crocus

Lyrics, Alan Hirsch

Melody, Alan Hirsch

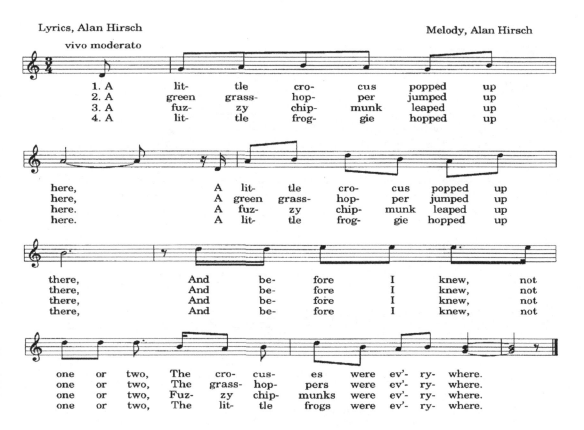

vivo moderato

1. A lit- tle cro- cus popped up
2. A green grass- hop- per jumped up
3. A fuz- zy chip- munk leaped up
4. A lit- tle frog- gie hopped up

here, A lit- tle cro- cus popped up
here, A green grass- hop- per jumped up
here. A fuz- zy chip- munk leaped up
here. A lit- tle frog- gie hopped up

there, And be- fore I knew, not
there, And be- fore I knew, not
there, And be- fore I knew, not
there, And be- fore I knew, not

one or two, The cro- cus- es were ev'- ry- where.
one or two, The grass- hop- pers were ev'- ry- where.
one or two, Fuz- zy chip- munks were ev'- ry- where.
one or two, The lit- tle frogs were ev'- ry- where.

This is another song by my former teaching colleague Alan Hirsch. To enliven this spring song, the adult can point to a child each time something in the song "pops up" and that child will then stand or hop up. On "everywhere" all the children can stand or hop up—but quickly go back again to be ready for the start of the next verse.

Lady Lichen and Mister Mossy

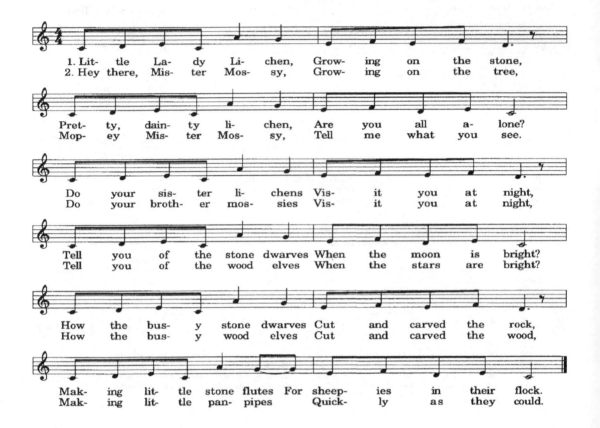

This diatonic song arose while contemplating the lichen and moss growing in a Colorado woodland. It is helpful to explain briefly the nature and growth habits of lichen and moss before beginning the song with children. My hope is that the song will bring this bit of nature lore to life for the children. The melody is fairly repetitious, partly to lull the singer into dreaminess. This makes if difficult to remember the "surprise" ending. The last phrase, "Quickly as they could," should be sung as quickly as humanly possible (by those who remember this!).

The Witch on a Windy Night

Lyrics, author unknown; with
additions by David Adams

Melody, David Adams

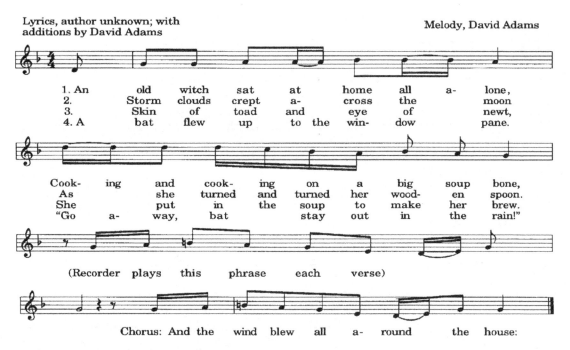

1. An old witch sat at home all a- lone,
2. Storm clouds crept a- cross the moon
3. Skin of toad and eye of newt,
4. A bat flew up to the win- dow pane.

Cook- ing and cook- ing on a big soup bone,
As she turned and turned her wood- en spoon.
She put in the soup to make her brew.
"Go a- way, bat stay out in the rain!"

(Recorder plays this phrase each verse)

Chorus: And the wind blew all a- round the house:

Shsheeeeeuuwh! (said while waving hands laterally to imitate wind)

5. A black cat came to her front door.
   "Go away, cat, I've chased you before!"

6. A dark, gray wolf stood by the gate.
   "Better get lost before it's too late!"

7. "You can all go hungry for all I care.
   Don't you know I hate to share?"

8. "I'll eat the soup myself," she sang.
   What happened? She exploded. BANG!

This responsive song (very appropriate for Halloween) features the adult singing the first, changing part of each verse, then playing the recorder phrase (or perhaps a child could play this), with the children singing the chorus and making the wind sound. Although the adult melody is in the key of F, the B natural in the chorus transposes the children's part into a pentatonic scale.

Puddle Huddle

Lyrics, Alan Hirsch and David Adams

Melody, David Adams

When we find a pud- dle, A- round it we may hud- dle. We

look in- to its mid- dle. We sing a lit- tle rid- dle:

How did the sky and I get in there, when all

the time we've been stand- ing here? We

see the face much like our own, We see the face and throw in a stone

And watch it rip- ple, rip- ple, And watch it rip- ple, rip- ple,

And then we go back home.

Wind Chimes

Lyrics, Alan Hirsch; adapted
by David Adams

Melody, Alan Hirsch; slightly
adapted by David Adams

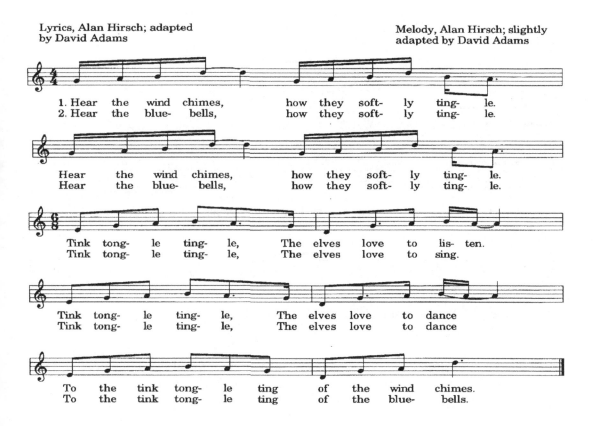

1. Hear the wind chimes, how they soft- ly ting- le.
2. Hear the blue- bells, how they soft- ly ting- le.

Hear the wind chimes, how they soft- ly ting- le.
Hear the blue- bells, how they soft- ly ting- le.

Tink tong- le ting- le, The elves love to lis- ten.
Tink tong- le ting- le, The elves love to sing.

Tink tong- le ting- le, The elves love to dance
Tink tong- le ting- le, The elves love to dance

To the tink tong- le ting of the wind chimes.
To the tink tong- le ting of the blue- bells.

Guardian Angel

Lyrics, Alois Künstler; translated
by Michael Blakemore and David Adams

Melody, Alois Künstler

Guard- dian an- gel, Watch me well Night and day,

Ear- ly and late, Till my soul trav- els through heav- en's bright gate.

(instrumental accompaniment) Guar- dian an- gel, Watch me well.

This song makes a lovely lullaby but can also be used for other occasions (for example, birthdays). Accompaniment by a lyre, harp or other stringed instrument adds to the "angelic" effect.

Processional Song for "The Fire on Tara"

Text, Eugene Schwartz

Melody, David Adams

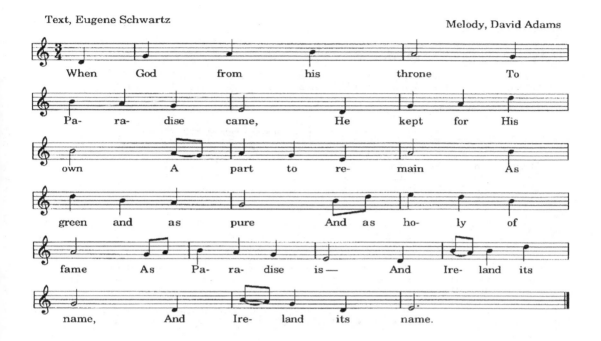

Soldier's Song

Text, Eugene Schwartz

Melody, David Adams

These two songs were composed for a second grade performance of Eugene Schwartz's play "The Fire on Tara." The attempt was made to create a pentatonic melody with an Irish feeling to it, as well as a martial feeling for the "Soldier's Song." The play can be found in the book Plays for Children and Communities by Eugene Schwartz (Rudolf Steiner College Publications, Fair Oaks, CA, 1992).

Down in the Barnyard

Southern Folk Song adapted and
expanded by David Adams

Briskly and energetically

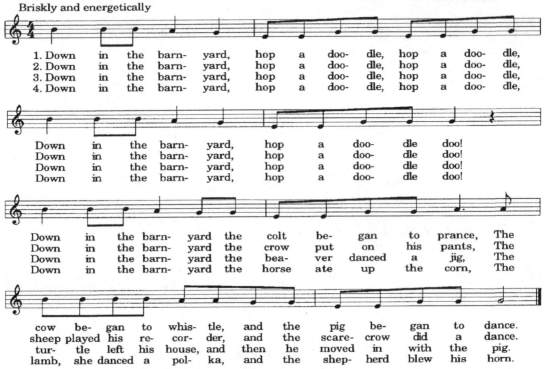

1. Down	in	the	barn-	yard,	hop	a	doo-	dle,	hop a doo- dle,
2. Down	in	the	barn-	yard,	hop	a	doo-	dle,	hop a doo- dle,
3. Down	in	the	barn-	yard,	hop	a	doo-	dle,	hop a doo- dle,
4. Down	in	the	barn-	yard,	hop	a	doo-	dle,	hop a doo- dle,

Down	in	the	barn-	yard,	hop	a	doo-	dle doo!
Down	in	the	barn-	yard,	hop	a	doo-	dle doo!
Down	in	the	barn-	yard,	hop	a	doo-	dle doo!
Down	in	the	barn-	yard,	hop	a	doo-	dle doo!

Down	in	the	barn-	yard	the	colt	be-	gan	to	prance, The
Down	in	the	barn-	yard	the	crow	put	on	his	pants, The
Down	in	the	barn-	yard	the	bea-	ver	danced	a	jig, The
Down	in	the	barn-	yard	the	horse	ate	up	the	corn, The

cow	be-	gan	to	whis-	tle,	and	the	pig be- gan to dance.
sheep	played his	re-	cor-	der,	and	the	scare-	crow did a dance.
tur-	tle	left	his	house,	and	then	he	moved in with the pig.
lamb,	she danced	a	pol-	ka,	and	the	shep-	herd blew his horn.

If sung with enough pace and knee-slapping liveliness, this infection tun will call to mind the plunking of a farmyard banjo, especially the "hop a doodle doo" sections. Please make up your own additional verses. The idea is to get a bit silly while still sticking to the barnyard theme. It's possible to be a little loose with the meter on the last line. Here are some other possibilities:

5. Down in the barnyard the dog fell asleep,
The cat lost her catnip, and she began to weep.

6. Down in the barnyard the farmer baked a pie,
The canary ate it all, but then he couldn't fly.

7. Down in the barnyard the owl began to hoot,
The sparrow stuffed his ears up, but the pig
danced in a boot.

8. Down in the barnyard the mouse put on a hat
The cat put on his coat. Now, what do you
think of that?

9. Down in the barnyard the chicken crossed the
path,
The goat rammed the water tank, and
everyone got a bath.

10. Down in the barnyard the fox stood on his head,
The hen walked a tightrope, and the farmer went to bed.

Song of Happiness

Lyrics and Melody, David Adams

Harmony, Carolyn Divine

This song was originally (1973) part of a multi-grade school play presenting the story of Pandora's Box. Due to the involvement of older children, it was not written in a pentatonic scale and was harmonized for piano accompaniment. It would be suitable for third grade children and older.

Columbus Day Song

The uncharacteristic topic of this song arose in answer to a child's question about the reason for the holiday of Columbus Day. It was originally accompanied by a story. Due to its more advanced historical content, I would not recommend this song for children younger than third grade, even though it uses a generally pentatonic melody. I intend for the "ahoy"s to be shouted rather than sung.

Three Beginning Recorder/Flute Songs – Grade 3

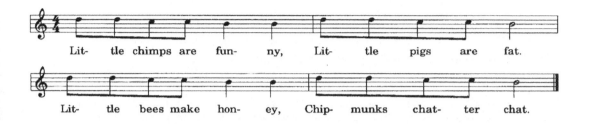

Lit- tle chimps are fun- ny, Lit- tle pigs are fat.

Lit- tle bees make hon- ey, Chip- munks chat- ter chat.

Come out- side and play with me While the sun shines fair.

We will find some daf- fo- dils To tie in our hair.

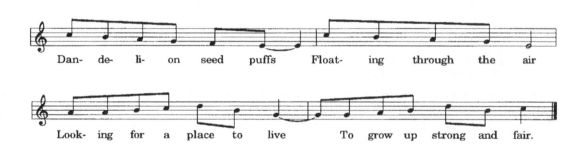

Dan- de- li- on seed puffs Float- ing through the air

Look- ing for a place to live To grow up strong and fair.

These three short pieces were designed for a somewhat unusual situation in Waldorf schools: a third grade transfer student who had never played the recorder or Choroi diatonic wooden flute (which is often introduced in third grade, replacing the pentatonic flute used earlier. The songs try to use the stepwise progression of the fingerings as much as possible while still retaining the child's interest. It is best to teach the child to sing the song first, so that it is well known before being attempted on the recorder.

Shepherds' Christmas Pageant

This assemblage of more or less familiar Christmas carols and spoken lines can be used as a simple Christmas pageant for a group of appropriately-costumed second or third grade children, loosely modeled after the medieval Shepherds' Play from Oberufer (an island on the Danube River).

SHEPHERDS [3 to 6 shepherds step forward from semicircle or row of all performers and sing the following song (by Michael Wilson), moving with appropriate gestures while singing]:

We are shep- herds and we sing of lots of jol- ly things. We can dance and we can shout; we can wave our caps a- bout. The stars shine a- bove us, the snow shines be- low, And we are so hap- py in this won- d'rous glow.

SHEPHERDS:
 We shepherds must rest, so down we lie
 To sleep a bit till day is nigh.

[Shepherds lie down and sleep. A group of angels steps forward and begins singing.]

1. From heav'n a- bove to earth we come To bear good news to ev- 'ry home; Glad ti- dings of great joy we bring, Where- of we now will say and sing:
2. To you this night is born a child Of Ma- ry, cho- sen vir- gin mild; This lit- tle child, of low- ly birth, Shall be the joy of all the earth.

FIRST SHEPHERD:
>   Shepherds, I dreamed of angels bright
>   Singing of a child born in the night.

SHEPHERDS:
>   We also heard this angel say.
>   Let's find the child 'ere break of day.

SECOND SHEPHERD:
>   We each must gifts to this child bring.
>   Though we're poor, we'll find something.

FIRST SHEPHERD: [Use as many gifts as there are shepherds, up to six]
>   A bottle of milk I will take.

SECOND SHEPHERD:
>   And I some flour for a cake.

THIRD SHEPHERD:
>   And I some eggs to help it bake.

FOURTH SHEPHERD:
>   And I soft wool,a pillow to make.

FIFTH SHEPHERD:
>   And I a fur, a blanket to make.

SIXTH SHEPHERD:
>   And I a rattle the child can shake.

[Shepherds walk off, circling the stage or performance area, to find the child, while instrumental music of the opening shepherds' song is played.]

[The shepherds arrive at the outside of the "stable," facing Mary, Joseph, and the child at the center of the row or semicircle of performers.]

SHEPHERDS:
>   Open the door, we pray.
>   Shepherds we are from far away.
>   We bend our knee; we bow our head.
>   We lay our gifts around his bed.

[While all the shepherds kneel, one by one, each shepherd brings his gift and lays it beside the cradle (or at the feet of Mary). While this is happening, everyone sings the following song as Mary gently rocks the child]

Lit- tle Je- sus, sweet- ly sleep, do not stir;

We will lend a coat of fur. We will rock you,

rock you, rock you. We will rock you, rock you, rock you.

See the fur to keep you warm, Snug- ly 'round your ti- ny form.

All children stand in a semi-circle facing the audience for this final song. The girls begin singing by themselves. The boys join in from the words "He came among us at Christmastide" to the end.

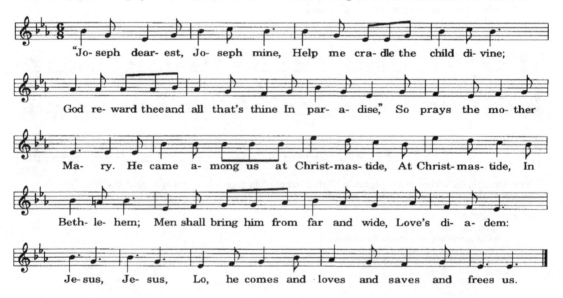

"Jo- seph dear- est, Jo- seph mine, Help me cra- dle the child di- vine;

God re- ward thee and all that's thine In par- a- dise," So prays the mo- ther

Ma- ry. He came a- mong us at Christ-mas- tide, At Christ- mas- tide, In

Beth- le- hem; Men shall bring him from far and wide, Love's di- a- dem:

Je- sus, Je- sus, Lo, he comes and loves and saves and frees us.

[A different Christmas carol could be used here if preferred — for example, "Silent Night."]

ALL [speaking to the audience with appropriate gestures]:
    You and I, I and you,
    We will give our light, too.

THE END

Made in the USA
Middletown, DE
19 February 2024

49790697R00051